CONSERVING RESOURCES

by Marne Ventura

Cody Koala

An Imprint of Pop!
popbooksonline.com

abdopublishing.com

Published by Pop!, a division of ABDO, PO Box 398166, Minneapolis, Minnesota 55439. Copyright © 2019 by POP, LLC. International copyrights reserved in all countries. No part of this book may be reproduced in any form without written permission from the publisher. Pop!™ is a trademark and logo of POP, LLC.

Printed in the United States of America, North Mankato, Minnesota

032018
092018

THIS BOOK CONTAINS RECYCLED MATERIALS

Distributed in paperback by North Star Editions, Inc.

Cover Photo: Shutterstock Images
Interior Photos: Shutterstock Images, 1, 5 (top), 5 (bottom left), 6, 9, 11, 13, 14–15, 17 (bottom right), 21 (middle); iStockphoto, 5 (bottom right), 17 (top), 17 (bottom left), 18, 21 (top), 21 (bottom)

Editor: Charly Haley
Series Designer: Laura Mitchell

Library of Congress Control Number: 2017963355

Publisher's Cataloging-in-Publication Data

Names: Ventura, Marne, author.
Title: Conserving resources / by Marne Ventura.
Description: Minneapolis, Minnesota : Pop!, 2019. | Series: Community economics |
Includes online resources and index.
Identifiers: ISBN 9781532160011 (lib.bdg.) | ISBN 9781635177961 (pbk) | ISBN 9781532161131 (ebook) |
Subjects: LCSH: Conservation of resources--Juvenile literature. | Community development--Juvenile literature. | Regional economics--Juvenile literature. | Economic development--Juvenile literature. | Community life--Juvenile literature.
Classification: DDC 330.9--dc23

Hello! My name is

Cody Koala

Pop open this book and you'll find QR codes like this one, loaded with information, so you can learn even more!

Scan this code* and others like it while you read, or visit the website below to make this book pop.

popbooksonline.com/conserving-resources

*Scanning QR codes requires a web-enabled smart device with a QR code reader app and a camera.

Table of Contents

Chapter 1

Natural Resources

People use resources from nature. They breathe air. They drink water. They eat food grown in soil.

Watch a video here!

People need fuel to power cars, heat their homes, and cook food. Oil, coal, and sunlight are some resources that people use to make fuel.

Coal, oil, and natural gas are called fossil fuels. They are formed from the remains of plants and animals that died a very long time ago.

The plants and animals that make up fossil fuels lived millions of years ago.

This machine is pumping oil out of the ground.

Conserving Resources

People need to save Earth's resources so there can be enough for everyone. This is called **conserving** resources.

The number of people in the world is growing. All must share Earth's resources.

Learn more here!

Save the Planet

Burning fossil fuels puts harmful gas into the air. Some factories and farms make harmful waste. Some waste goes into the soil and water.

Learn more here!

The soil, water, and air are becoming less healthy. Earth is filling up with people's trash. Old toys, cans, and bottles are buried in landfills.

People need to keep Earth
healthy. That way Earth can
keep providing resources.

Chapter 4

Reduce, Reuse, Recycle

People can **reduce**, **reuse**, and **recycle** to conserve resources.

Complete an activity here!

To reduce means to use less of a resource. Turning the light off when leaving a room uses less electricity.

Reusing a lunchbox makes less trash than using paper bags.

Recycling means turning trash into something new. People can give aluminum cans to a recycling center. The cans will be recycled into new cans.

Reduce
Kelly turns off the faucet after she's done getting water.

Reuse
John writes on the back side of used paper.

Recycle
Thomas puts a plastic bottle in the recycling bin.

Making Connections

Text-to-Self

How can you conserve resources at home or school?

Text-to-Text

Have you read about reducing, reusing, and recycling before? How was it similar to what you read here? How was it different?

Text-to-World

How have you seen people conserve resources in your neighborhood?

Glossary

conserving – saving something and not wasting it.

fossil fuel – fuel made from the remains of plants and animals that died millions of years ago.

recycle – to make trash into something that can be used.

reduce – to use less of something.

resource – something that people use to live.

reuse – to use something again.

Index

Online Resources

popbooksonline.com

Thanks for reading this Cody Koala book!

Scan this code* and others like it in this book, or visit the website below to make this book pop!

popbooksonline.com/conserving-resources

*Scanning QR codes requires a web-enabled smart device with a QR code reader app and a camera.